"No great mind has existed without a touch of madness."
-Aristotle

I should start off by saying that I'm not very good at judging distance or symmetry or the facial reconstruction of celebrities. I can't quite put my finger on the disease or the way rims of glasses always drop when I drink and I tend to spill all over my clothes and all over the floor and all over everything. It's not my fault that I take the blame, it's easier, more precise, and we can all move on. It was all my fault, hang me up, shoot me down, shock me out of life I don't give a damn as long as everyone else is happy and satisfied with how things are going. I make spelling errors and mix up my grammar and hate the way my toes are always too warm in socks and shoes and boots and winter and I hate the way I hate the way I say things. People don't always understand how often I take to my encyclopedia of dictionaries. Not because I'm a pretentious asswagon (although I am) but because it's the only thing I have left from her. I wonder what would have happened if it had been the other way around. I'm sure she would have been grand to have around right about now when the world is crashing in and I am imploding in on myself. I make a black hole and the last thing I want is to pull you in, but if it takes us back in time I think I could change. I'm not sure if I want to.

The emergency waiting room at University Hospital reeked of fear. It burned my nostrils and gutted my stomach. As I sit here, intestines exposed, ready to be scaled, I've lost it. Of everyone, the boy who ate the pavement on his skateboard, the obese lady vomiting a concoction of blo[od], broken teeth, the obvious appendix patient they left scuff marks on the floor for, everyone [is here for] me. The girl who can't stop shaking and crying and damning Danny Bonaduce. Somehow the main event.

"Are you sure I'm an emergency?" I whimper out to my mother, who is [doing] well under the circumstances. She didn't answer at first, wrapping her shou[lders in a] bulking mass of tears.

"Yes, darling," she whispers, "of course you are." I can't quit[e]

The security guard adjusts his black cloak as my eyes blur h[im] and rolled in chain-mail and painted-black metal. A dark warrior [comes] out as my eyes clear I see him true. The chain-mail falling aro[und him] too many years on the force. I tell him to go home to his fa[mily]

"Wow, Prince Harry got hot," my mother comme[nts on] royalty flying an army jet. "He wasn't even the cute or[e]"

I sputter out a laugh, "He's hot, but ging' can't [be] comfort of royalty is artificial and all I have. In my m[ind I] [fir]st [woul]d take apart this chain and...

"Why not?"

And slit my wrists with the screws, "'Cause! [people] would think we're brother and sister!" I explain furio[usly]. [My] whole god damn life building is fragile and fatigued. T[he]

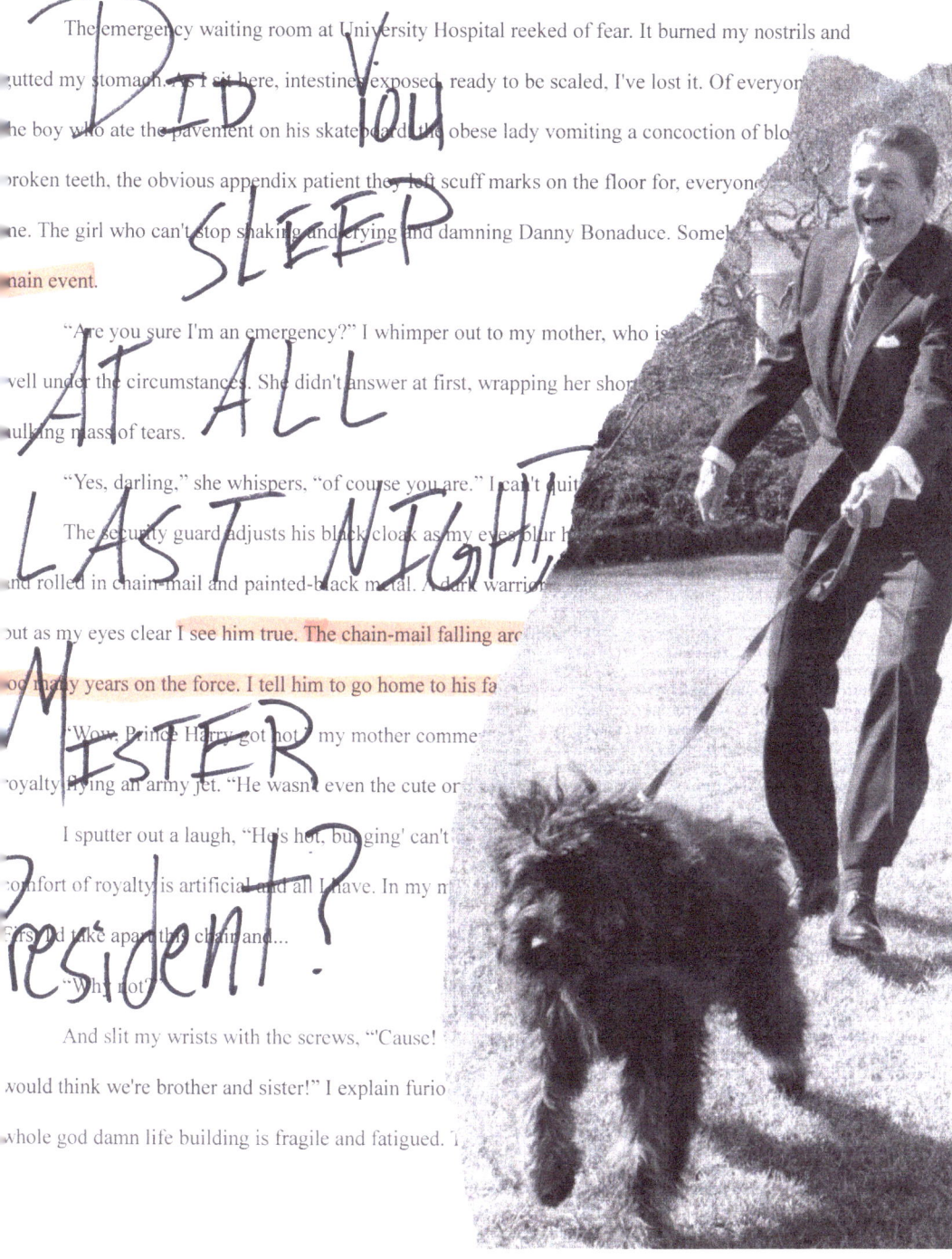

Handwritten overlay: DID YOU SLEEP AT ALL LAST NIGHT, MISTER PRESIDENT?

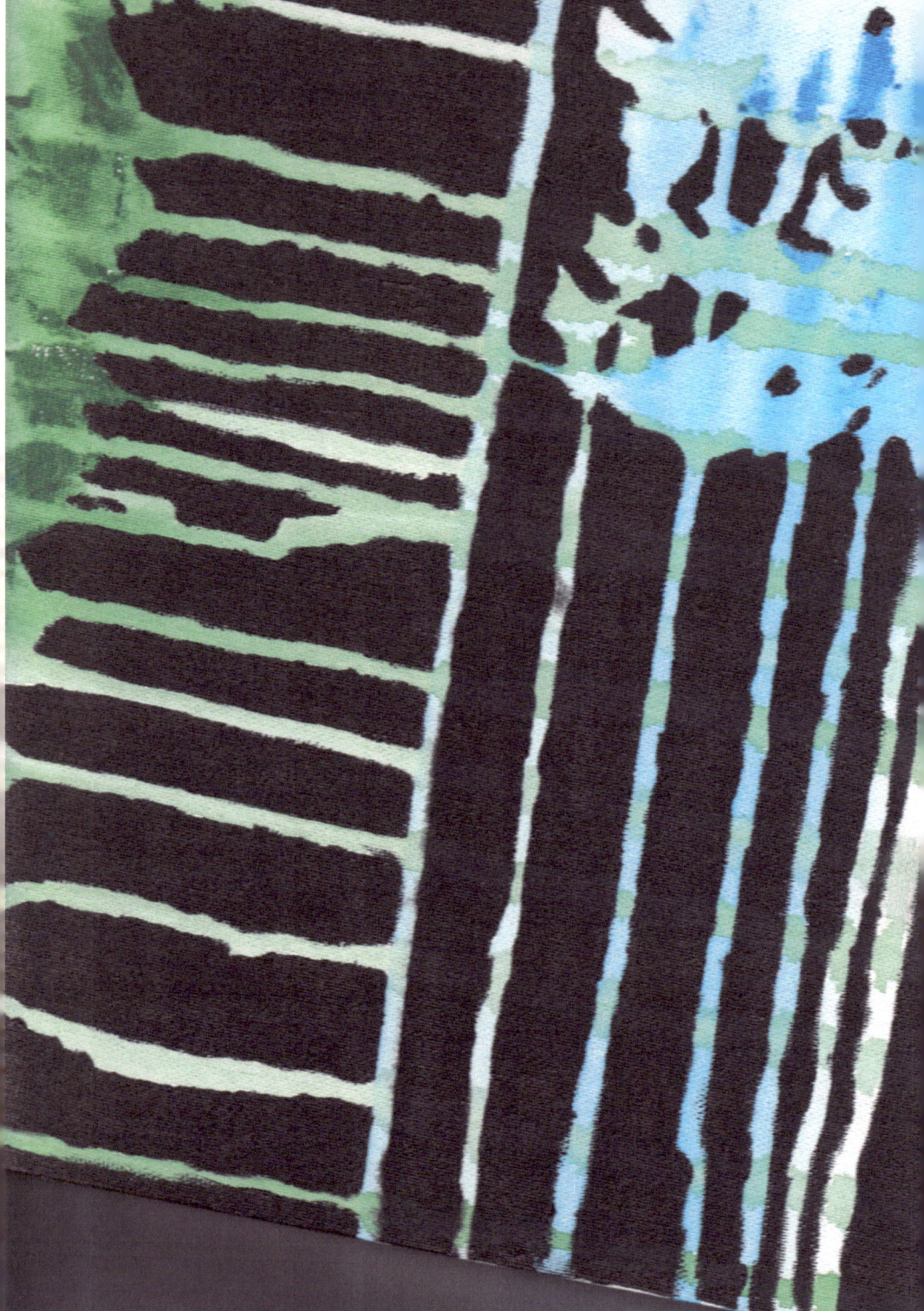

You broke your crown
but that's ok, you still have the throne
you think
or maybe you were murdered in your sleep
by a macbeth wanna be
either way
at least you'll be remembered.

Live on, Duncan, live on.

Studio - Madison, WI
  -$565 minimum
  *Plan for $800/month
Equipment:
  -Acoustics for Room
    :Acoustic Foam
      -Grid 2"x66"x43", 2"x69", 45"
        $2"x66" x 43" = $63.99
      *Plan for $200
  - Microphones
    1. Large
      : Stu
        -                         4/2020
        **$89.95 -$99.00
    2. Microphone Clamp Filter ✓ 4/23/
      : Nady MPF -6 (6
        - $12.59
Production   Costs
  : qualityrecordpressings.com
    543 N. 10th St.
    Salina, Kansas 6T
  :12" Regular Weight
    -500-999 $1.35 eac   —$134
    * $700 budget
  :Easy Disc.net
    -$85 -$200 Jewel c   -100

Is this
what you
want from me?

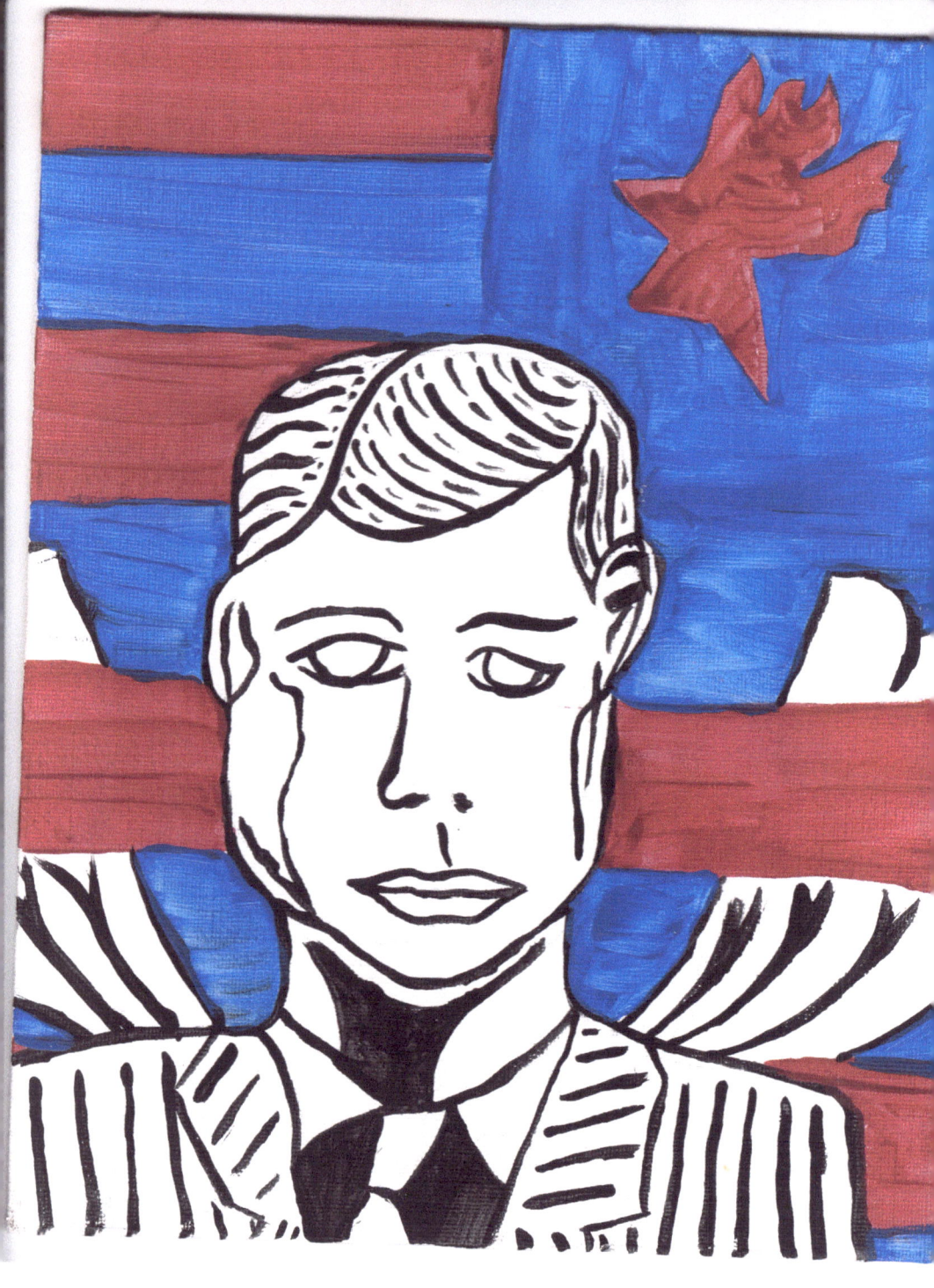

BA / BS Degree Requirements
COLLEGE OF LETTERS & SCIENCE

Effective for students matriculating to any postsecondary institution as of May 21, 2007, and later or who opted into the 2007 degree requirements

TOOLS for Learning and Communication

University General Education Requirements

One Quantitative Reasoning A course (q)
One Quantitative Reasoning B course (r)
One 3- credit Ethnic Studies course (e)

One Communication A course (a)
One Communication B course (b)

Mathematics

Bachelor of Arts	Bachelor of Science
Meet QR-A OR Quantitative A & B above	Two 3- credit courses at I'A level (MATH. COMP SCI STAT Limit one each: COMP SCI STAT)

Foreign Language

Bachelor of Arts	Bachelor of Science
Fourth level of a language, **or** Third level of a language **and** Second level of another language	Third level of a language

BREADTH of Exploration in the Liberal Arts & Sciences

Humanities: 12 credits (L,H,X,Z)
— Must include 6 credits Literature, L

Social Science: 12 credits (S,W,Y,Z)

Natural Science: 12 credits (B,P,N,W,X,Y)

Bachelor of Arts	Bachelor of Science
One 3- credit Biological Science course (B) One 3- credit Physical Science course (P)	6 credit Physical Science (P) 6 credit Biological Science (B)

108 Liberal Arts & Sciences credits (C)

DEPTH of Inquiry in the Liberal Arts & Sciences

Mastery of Intermediate/Advanced level work A,I,A,D

Major: Declare at least one major

QUANTITY & QUALITY of work

120 Total Credits
UW–Madison Experience
    30 credits in **residence** overall
    30 credits in **residence** after the 60th credit

Minimum GPAs
    2.0 in all courses at UW–Madison
    2.0 in I,A,D-level work at UW–Madison

    level credits in residence in each major
    campus in each major department

2.0 in all major & major department courses
2.0 in upper-level major & major courses

This is not a degree audit. For accurate degree progress information, consult DARS. Students are encouraged to exceed minimum requirements. There are limits on certain kinds of credits — consult DARS for more information.

I CANT GO BACK IN OR IT WILL KILL ME

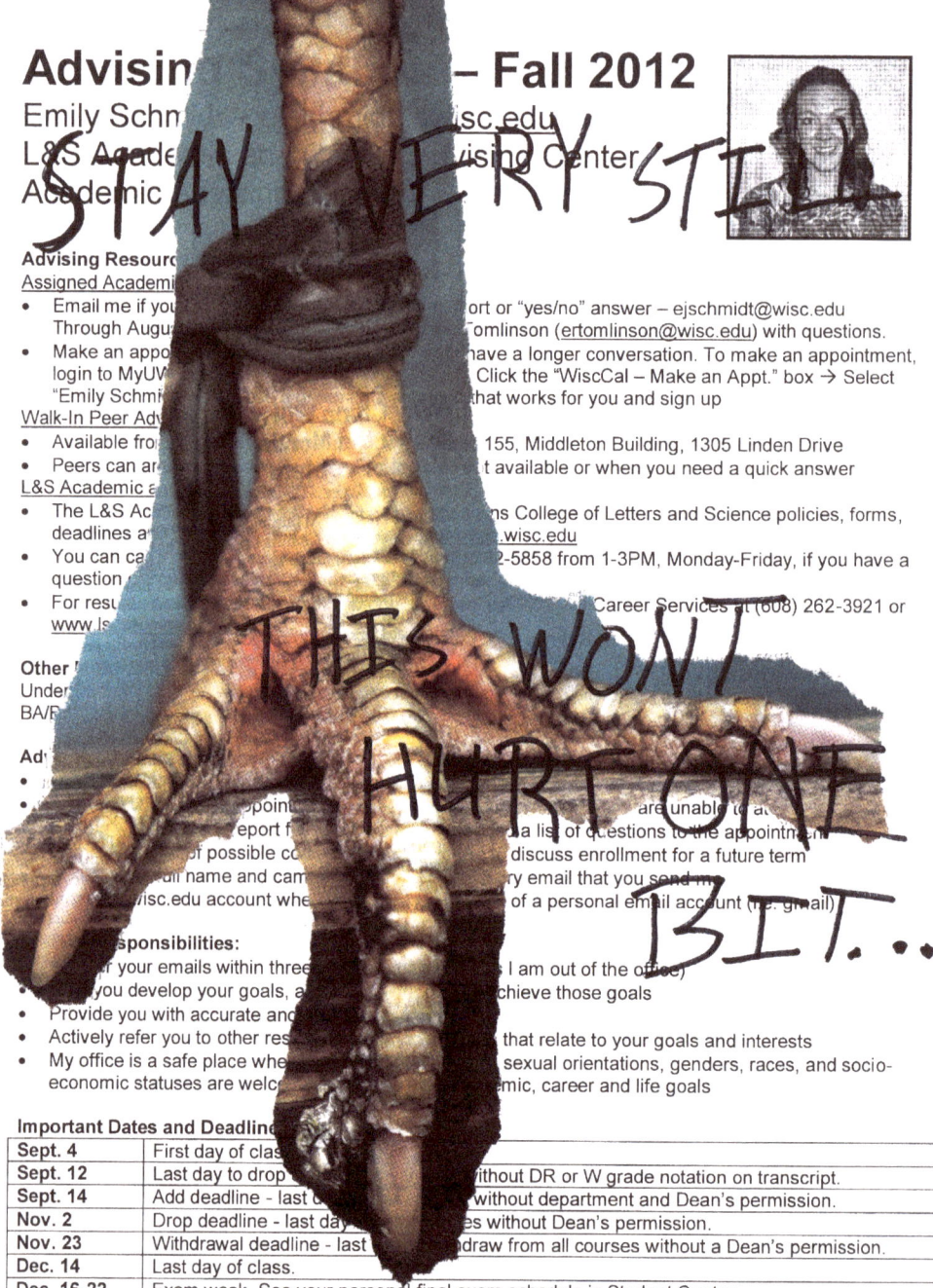

Advisin... – Fall 2012

Emily Schm... ...isc.edu
L&S Acade... ...ising Center
Academic...

STAY VERY STILL

Advising Resour...
Assigned Academi...
- Email me if you... ...ort or "yes/no" answer – ejschmidt@wisc.edu
  Through Augu... ...omlinson (ertomlinson@wisc.edu) with questions.
- Make an appo... ...have a longer conversation. To make an appointment,
  login to MyUW... ...Click the "WiscCal – Make an Appt." box → Select
  "Emily Schmi... ...that works for you and sign up

Walk-In Peer Ad...
- Available fro... ...155, Middleton Building, 1305 Linden Drive
- Peers can ar... ...t available or when you need a quick answer

L&S Academic a...
- The L&S Ac... ...ns College of Letters and Science policies, forms,
  deadlines a... ...wisc.edu
- You can ca... ...2-5858 from 1-3PM, Monday-Friday, if you have a
  question...
- For resu... ...Career Services at (608) 262-3921 or
  www.ls...

Other ...
Under...
BA/...

Ad...
- ...
- ...point... ...are unable to a...
  ...eport f... ...a list of questions to the appointm...
  ...possible co... ...discuss enrollment for a future term
  ...all name and cam... ...ry email that you send m...
  ...isc.edu account whe... ...of a personal email account (ie. gmail)

THIS WON'T HURT ONE BIT...

...sponsibilities:
- ...r your emails within three... ...I am out of the office)
- ...you develop your goals, a... ...chieve those goals
- Provide you with accurate and...
- Actively refer you to other res... ...that relate to your goals and interests
- My office is a safe place whe... ...sexual orientations, genders, races, and socio-
  economic statuses are welc... ...mic, career and life goals

Important Dates and Deadline...

Sept. 4	First day of clas...
Sept. 12	Last day to drop... ...ithout DR or W grade notation on transcript.
Sept. 14	Add deadline - last d... ...without department and Dean's permission.
Nov. 2	Drop deadline - last day... ...es without Dean's permission.
Nov. 23	Withdrawal deadline - last... ...draw from all courses without a Dean's permission.
Dec. 14	Last day of class.
Dec. 16-22	Exam week. See your personal final exam schedule in Student Center.

I am looking forward to seeing you this semester. Best wishes for a successful fall term!

You all lied to me
You said I'd feel better in the morning.

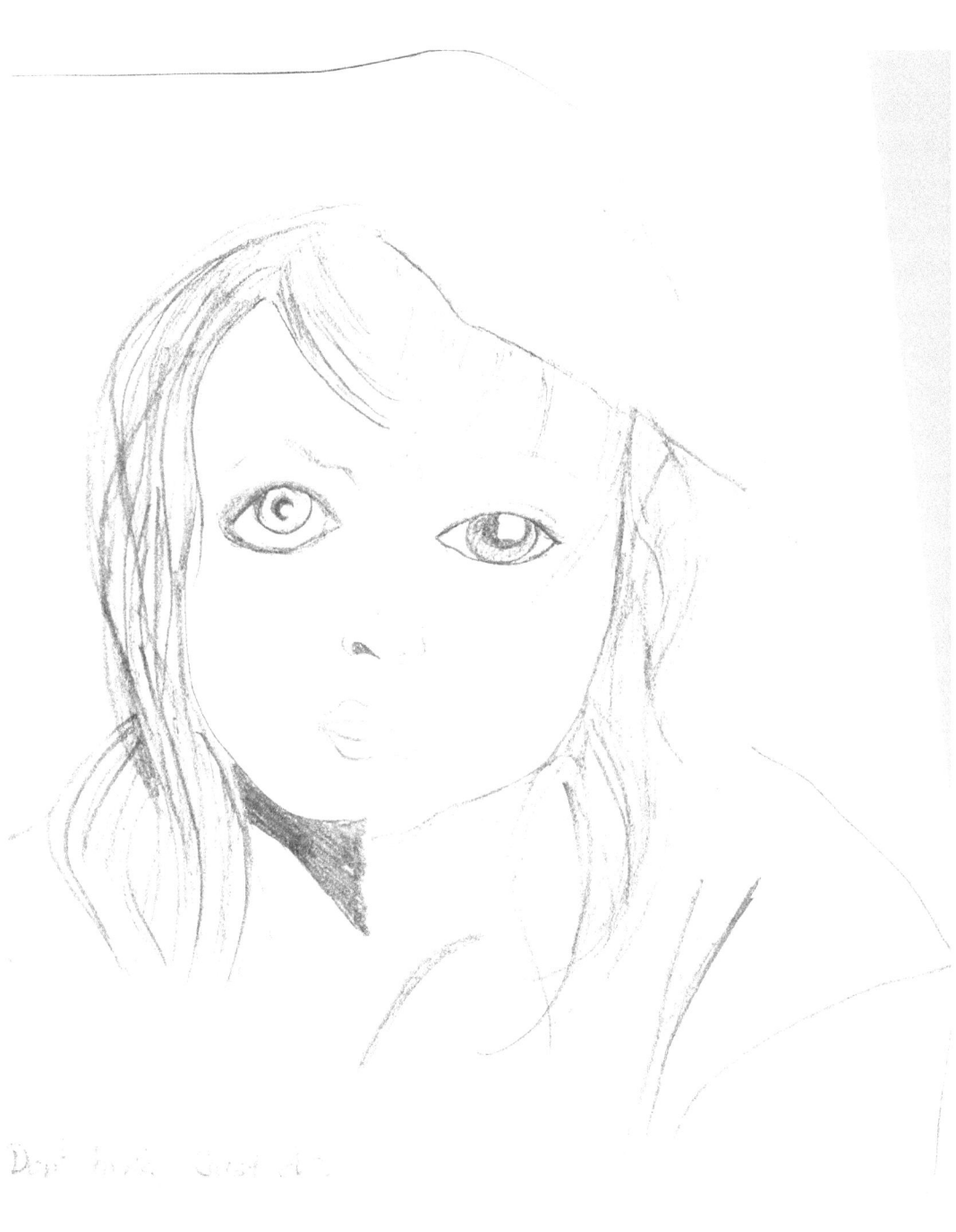

Data? Data? Where'd you run off to?
We have to find him, Captain. We must.
He could be hurt. He could be dead!

Tasha, he's a fucking droid.

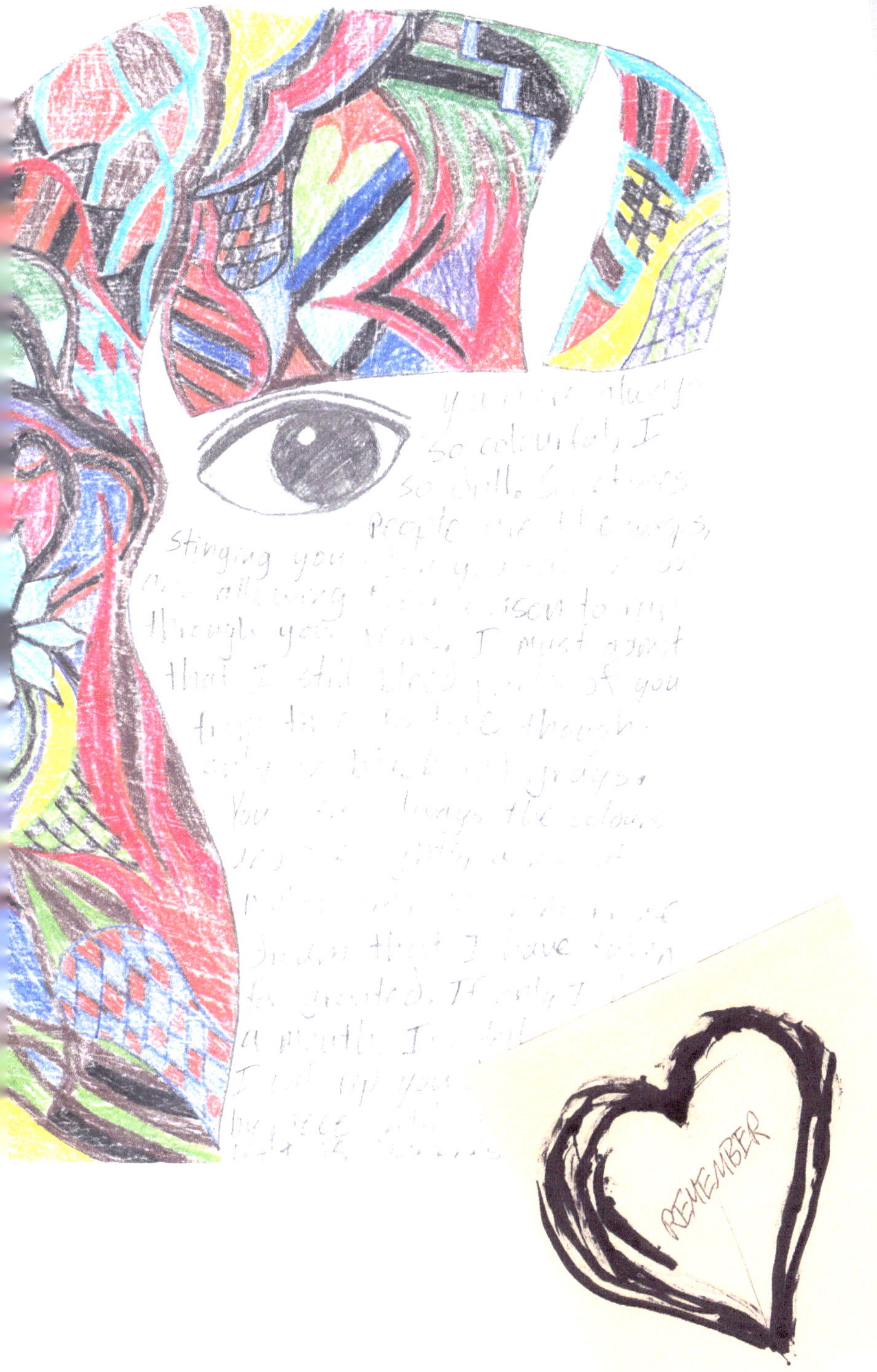
so colourful, I
Stinging you
I must admit
REMEMBER

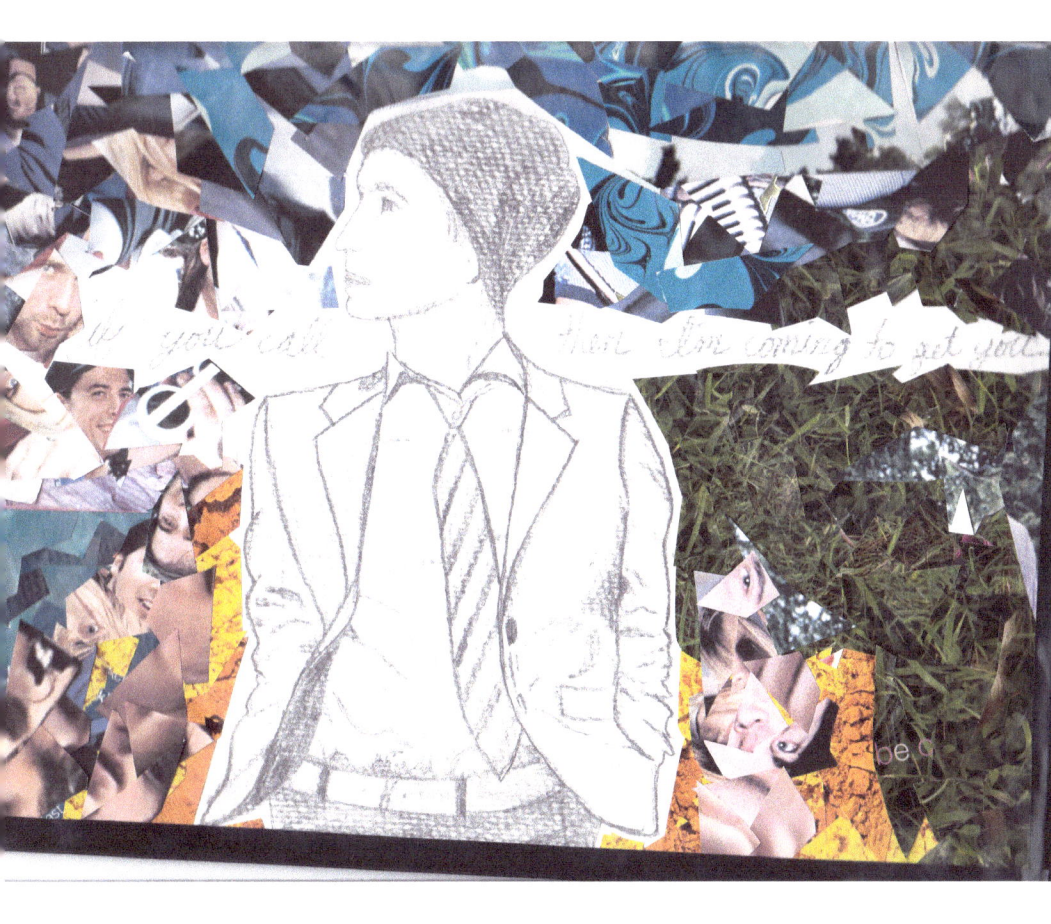

PAIN.
IF YOU
MAKE IT
BEAUTIFUL,
DOES IT
GO
AWAY?

I learned in English that I speak a different language completely my own and no one could understand the way I spoke. I used too many words, too many metaphors. It hurt when I realized that they couldn't see what I could see. They didn't see the same blues or reds or greens. I saw the light, they saw the matter.

I don't want to let me look after...

I don't want to talk about my...

Don't ever send me back to the hospital
...want to talk again
Don't send me back to the hospital
This time I want to...

...that I need to do
...me back...
...this away
...shout the rocks out of my stomach
...before...
...think too much

So what you're saying is that you're saying nothing at all
I already knew that

Roles Now

Person - I contribute to society as an individual part of a whole

Daughter - I contribute to a family in hopes of future prosperity

Sister - I contribute to my brothers as a unit that both gives and needs support and love.

Student - I dedicate myself to my studies in hopes of future prosperity and contribution to society

Roommate - I contribute to building relationships and keep a livable situation.

Friend - I am available to give and receive support, guidance, and advice.

Rockstar - I actively dedicate myself to my arts in hop of future and present prosperity and happiness.

Personal Mission Statement.

I vow to live my life compassionately, passionately and with an open mind in order to dedicate myself to my passions and personal happiness while also aiding in the pursuit of passions and personal happiness of others.

How?

- I will listen more often than I speak, really truly listen and understand the ideas of others.

- I will allow my heart to guide me on my path and dedicate myself fully to what makes me happy.

- I will remember the importance of every individual I meet and ~~learn~~ learn something from each.

I will live in the present, but not without planning for the future, keeping the end in mind.

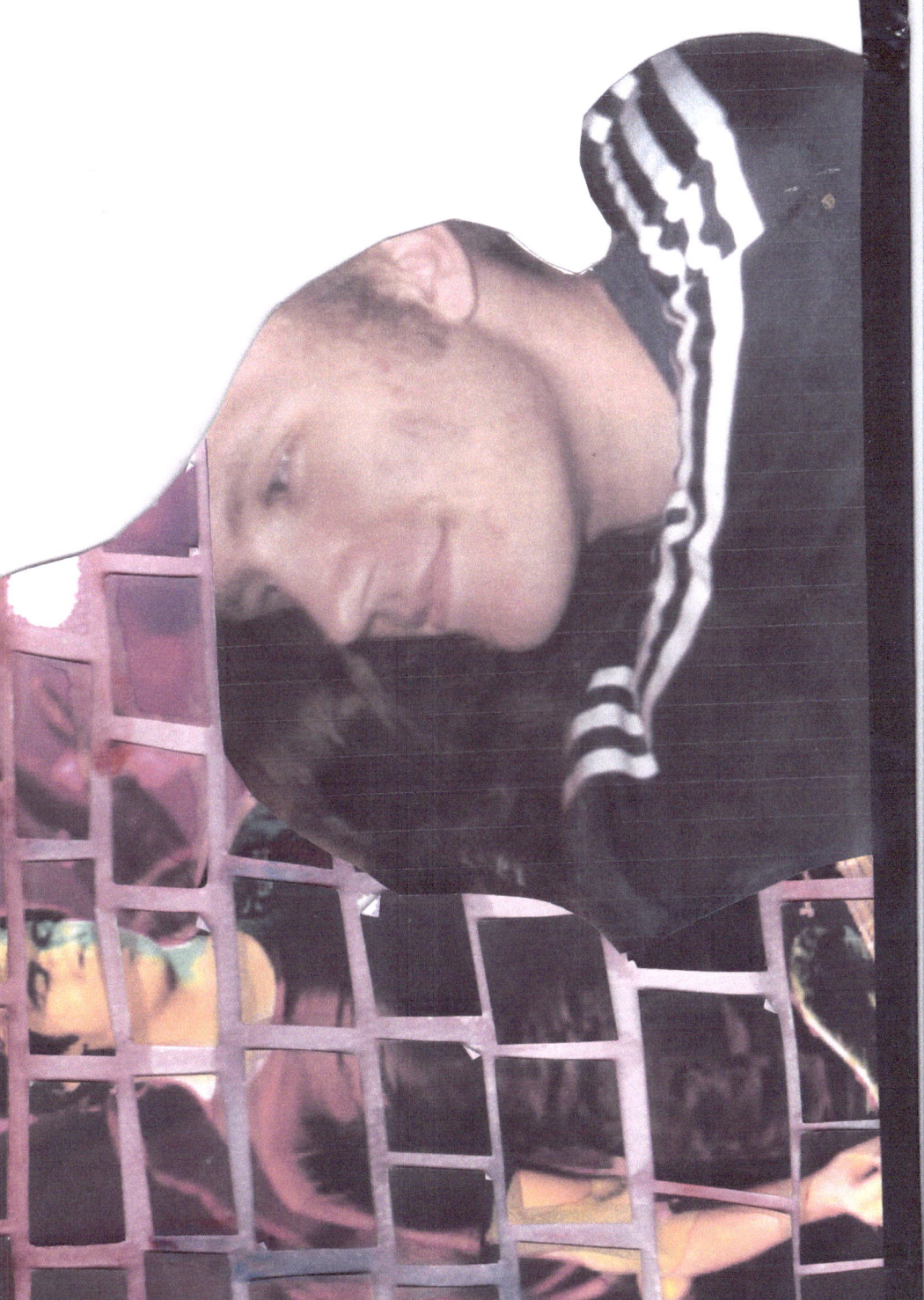

A. Danger Ross - Delusions of Grandeur
1. Silence itself
2. Enterprise
3. Mark David Chapman → Don't know
4. ~~George Heresy~~ BTK
5. Friendly Fire   about the double
Bonus: Jesse's Flowers → same thing...

Songs

Enterprise   - Mark David Chapman
Silence itself   - Lee Harvey Oswald
Sunshine (WT)   - Whoever shot Bobby
George Heresy (DB eyes)   (suri-suri?)
Jesse's Flowers /or/ Friendly Fire   or was that
                                      Reagan? or did I
                                      just Make that up

Enterprise you ween in and out of my life ~

Pain Pain Pain   Pain

I was beautiful like lightening is you make it
you were thundering behind) beautiful
But when I hit the ground does it go away?
you stayed in the sky

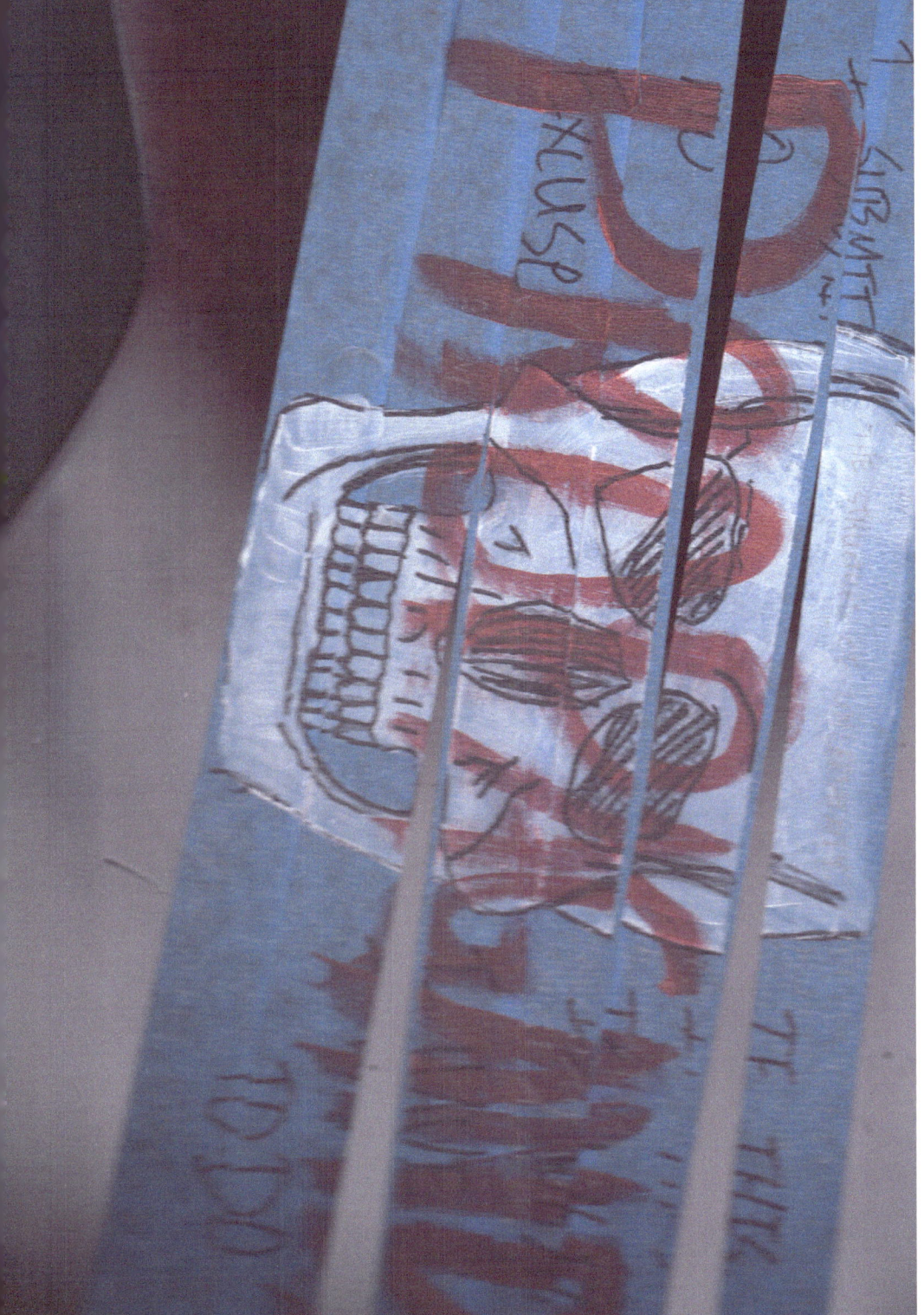

You wake up sick. As always. Rifle through your bag of empty pill bottles and Pepto-Bismol. Take one from each full container. Even the vitamins. Your mind's in shambles, but at least your hair looks nice. Or it will once you shower. And blow dry. And straighten. Your nail polish is chipped and you wonder why you even bothered, although you know it was because you wanted your hands to be pretty when you didn't feel very pretty at all. You play the Breakfast Club for the umpteenth time and try to eat but it just wont go down and you just can't get up. Feed the fish. He eats. He can always eat. You're so jealous you consider starving him. Or not cleaning his bowl. But you don't want to kill him. He's the only one there, awake with you at four in the morning. Him and the birds. The medication smells like rain but it falls like hail and you smash into the pavement. Not the pavement, your bed. It only feels like it's made with concrete.

ART

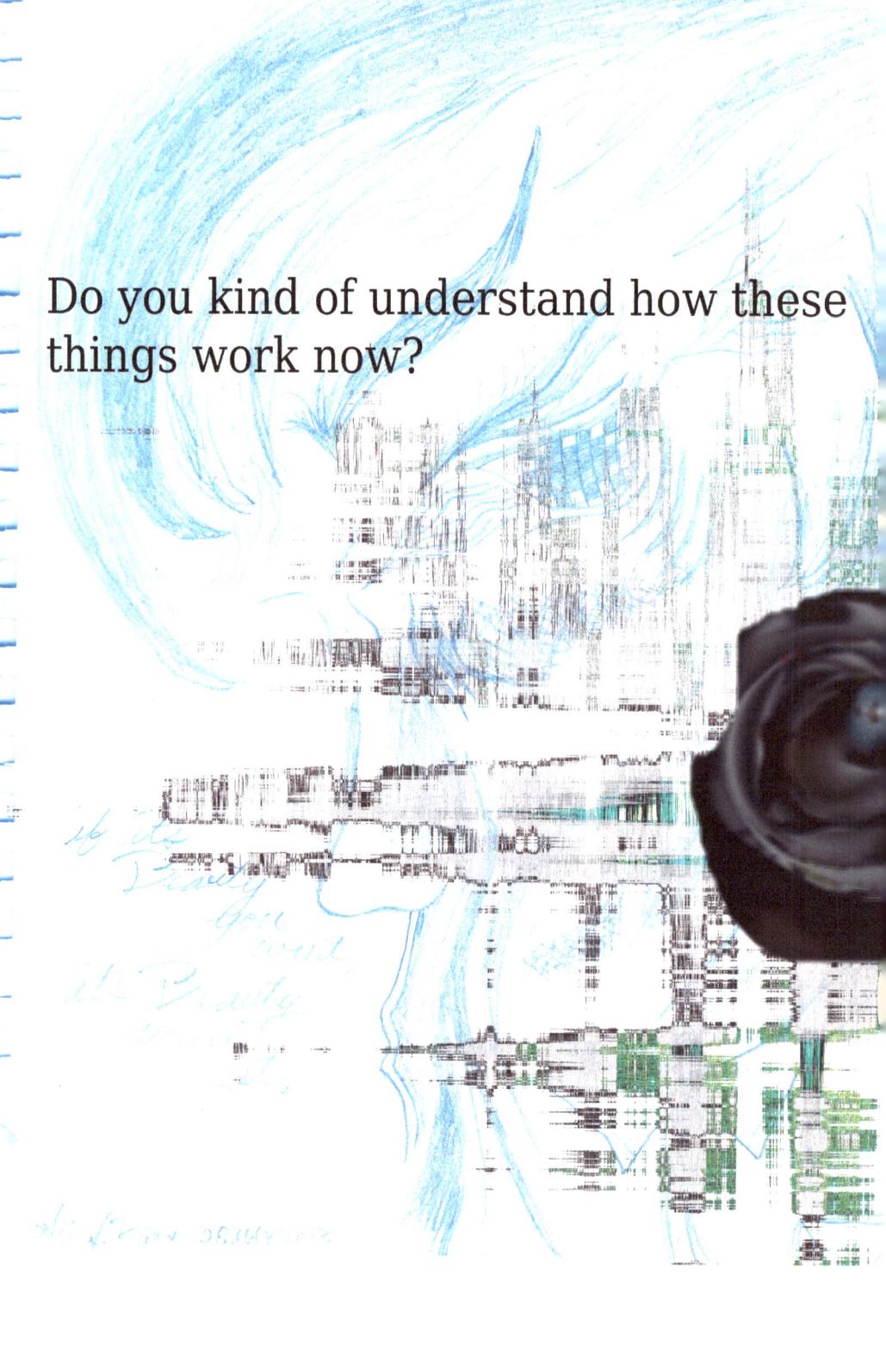

Do you kind of understand how these things work now?

A special thanks

- to the terrible education system
- to the men who built the fence wrong (measure twice, cut once, boys)
- to awful parents who hate their kids
- to awful kids who hate their parents
- to awful people who are awful
- to shitty weather
- to the inconsistencies of the English language
- to the inconsistencies of my personality
- to the inconsistencies of my thought patterns
- to my lack of talent
- to my lack of attention span
- to my lack of serotonin
- to my excessive over thinking
- to my excessive under-doing
- to my excessive obsessions
- to stubbed toes
- to hang nails
- to running out of coffee
- to not running as much as I should
- to running late
- to being late for my own events
- to george harrison's tumours
- to mark david chapman's bullets
- to these bullet points
- to my pretention
- to my illusion of safety
- to my illusion of danger
- to my allusions to Star Trek
- to my allusions to Greek mythology
- to my greek heritage
- to my irish heritage
- to my german heritage
- to my untamed hair
- to my dry hands
- to my callouses
- to my blisters
- to looking into the sun

"If God gave me grace, then why aren't I graceful?"
-Jesse Lacey

www.ingramcontent.com/pod-product-compliance
Lightning Source LLC
Chambersburg PA
CBHW041118180526
45172CB00001B/303